Internal Demons
By: B.J.A.S

Table of Contents

For:
The Abused
The Addict
The Broken
The Brave
The Forgotten
The Failure
The Hero
The Heartbroken
The Innocent
The Invisible
The Loner
The Lost
The One Hiding In The Shadow
The Overcomer
The Self-Harmer
The Survivor

These are all for you.

My mind loves to over think,
in turn my heart tends to sink.
Maybe I should see a shrink,
cause it's pushing me to the brink.

How do I keep going,
in my eyes the pain is showing.
My smiles stopped glowing,
and my laughs are slowing.

I keep pushing the tears away,
they don't miss a day.
I even got on my knees to pray,
but the devil loves to play.

I try to take a step back,
and look over the facts.
Mind picks up the slack,
emotions quick to overreact.

Try to stay on a positive note,
but I can barely keep my head afloat.
I had sought the antidote,
in the words people spoke.

What I've had to endure,
shows in the strength I procure.
My intentions are pure,
happiness unable to secure.

In pursuit of peace,
expectations I've had to release.
Depression seeks to increase,
while I plead for it to cease.

Life consists of trials and tribulations,
it's built my moral foundations.
Focusing on manifestations,
instead of the limitations.

~Pursuit

Constantly looking for a way to cope,
with the thoughts in my head.
Holding on to that thing we call hope,
you'll be okay they said.

But when do they stop,
the demons that speak?
Get on top,
they love to shriek.

From the start,
they've tore into my mind.
Tearing apart,
any peace I happen to find.

But there is a voice,
telling me not to give in.
It says I have a choice,
to push away the demons within.

The voice that I hear,
is what I call my will to survive.
But the demons make me fear,
and question why I'm even alive.

~Will to survive

There are to many days,
where I have to force a smile.
May need to change my ways,
am I stuck in denial?

How do you explain,
when you don't even know why?
All I can do is bear the pain,
and try not to cry.

But they don't comprehend,
the level of discontent with my life.
How much I must pretend,
that I don't want to pick up a knife.

How much I must act,
like I care if I die.
When in fact,
I must beg myself not to cut open my thigh.

You would flee,
if you seen the darkness in my mind.
But this is me,
you won't be happy with what you find.

But if I scare you away,
please don't come back.
That's where you need to stay,
if I want to keep the broken me intact.

I don't want to ever,
fall in love again.
Because there is no forever,
and I'm tired of missing what we could've been.

I'm tired of wiping my eyes,
and blowing my nose.
I'm tired of the goodbyes,
this isn't what I chose.

So ill stay to myself,
and hope for the best.
Grab the blunt of the shelf,
ease the sadness in my chest.

~All an act

Losing my soul,
out of control.
Pain takes a toll,
far from being whole.

Look in my eye,
what do you see?
It's not me,
I don't know this Bri.

I remember that girl,
who would spin and twirl.
Her laughs came in a whirl,
passionate heart she'd unfurl.

Herself she had to isolate,
from the world and its weight.
She would assimilate,
All the sadness and hate.

She couldn't help but feel,
the pain her mother would instill.
The tragedies way to real,
she got a sad but raw deal.

Tried to keep her head elevated,
but to often she went unappreciated.
Innocence was annihilated,
to live or to die she contemplated.

~The Old Me

Everyday is a fight,
to do what's right.
To seek out the light,
and not take flight.

The pain my own to bare,
this I refuse to share.
For I remain aware,
that life is far from fair.

I seek freedom,
to rule my own kingdom.
Flee away from boredom,
towards attaining wisdom.

Humans have the toxic trait,
to use false love as bait.
Pushing your heart to hate,
saying just accept your fate.

We take on this role,
that focuses on control.
Just to fill a dark hole,
that's embedded in our soul.

Quick to fake a smile,
it's become a trending style.
Loneliness is why we reconcile,
relationships that are vile.

~False Love

It's clear that we're not alright,
still you're the only one in my sight.
I don't know why we have to fight,
or how it came to saying things out of spite.

See I know we'll get through the bad days,
that all these doubts are just a phase.
I'll do my best to give you your praise,
and I'll always revel in your gaze.

I won't leave us up to fate,
because by then we might be to late.
You're the last person I could think to hate,
and I do my best not to berate.

-Yours Always

Do you know the despair of the night,
the heartache of the fight?
How about the hope of the light,
or the smiles that shine bright?

See you can't have the good without the bad,
the happy without the sad.
You can't have the calm without the mad,
and you can't focus on what you could have had.

You have to hit a low,
to get to the point you seek to grow.
Expectations you have to stow,
and gratitude you have to show.

At times you need to quiet your mind,
look inside and deal with what you find.
You can't let your anger blind,
you have to get on your grind.

Yes, sometimes you got to walk that extra mile,
just so you can smile.
And when your body's feeling vile,
you have to make yourself get off that tile.

You have to push to be the best,
and not settle for mediocrity like the rest.
You have to feel it in your chest,
but know that you're always blessed.

~The Balance

I hate the day I met you,
you let my feelings brew.

Memories I want to let go,
my love I have to stow.
But it just comes to show,
that you don't have me when I'm low.

Aren't given me your time,
even when you know I'm a dime.
This must be a sign,
that we will never shine.

These feelings I repress,
and thoughts of me you suppress.
You're a person I wont even stress,
with my love, you I tried to bless.

You tried to make me feel like I was a disgrace,
especially after the times you would kiss on my face.
You just wanted to feel all up on my lace,
and wrap your hands around my waist.

But now I finally see,
that there will never be a we.
Cause you were never down for me,
even after times you promised you would be.

I wasted so much time,
on a nigga who wasn't even mine.
Steady tryna get you off my mind,
but my hearts in a bind.

So many excuses I would make,
to keep you in my life but I know that's a mistake.
All thoughts of you I'm constantly trying to shake,
and when I can't I kind of want to drown myself in
a lake.

How did we go from laughing and walking around
the mall,
to now you hitting ignore every time that I fucking
call?
The act of something so small,
when I hear your voicemail, I can't help but feel my
heart fall.

I can feel you praying for me to fail,
but I'm out here still wishing for you to prevail.
And all that bullshit you would sale,
should put a post card on it and sent it back in the
fucking mail.

I'm not someone you can compare,
at me these niggas stare.
I just wanted you to care,
but you just wanted to hurt and tear.

Let the cards fall where they may,
however, there will be a day,
That you regret ever pushing me away,
when you should have been begging for me to stay.

Years down the road you will miss,
the touch and feel of my kiss.
And you will hate that now they are all his,
you should have enjoyed when I was wrapped up in
your ignorant bliss.

Crazy thing is I would have walked miles,
just to see you fucking smile.
Instead I'm laying here on the tile,
with my body feeling kind of vile.

I guess to love you is wrong,
got to keep my head up and stay strong.
This has gone on for way to long,
so I'ma leave these feelings here at the end of this
fucking song.

~Played Yourself

So to me,
this is all fucked up and strange.
Because what I see,
is the way you switch up and change.

You said you'd be here,
but you're no where to be found.
Now my hearts full of fear,
and my back against the ground.

We took it at a fast pace,
had our heads in a cloud.
But I swore I'd never chase,
I just wanted to be wowed.

Shoulda kept you at a distance,
and never let you in my bed.
Over my head I feel your absence,
fuck everything that you said.

Wanted to beg why,
but I have an immense amount of pride.
I don't want to cry,
so, I pushed the tears to side.

My mind keeps wandering,
to thoughts of you smiling.
You got me over here pondering,
why the fuck do you keep on lying?

~Reverse Card

It's Valentine's Day,
and I really want to cry.
Fuck every word you would say,
but at least I can say I try.

I don't want hearts,
and I don't want flowers.
I want to make art,
with another nigga in the shower.

How does it make you feel?
me being with someone new.
Now it's more real,
and I hope you're feeling blue.

~Rebound

I'm constantly counting down the days,
just know the distance is a phase.
And it might sound like a cliché,
but I can't wait to shower you with praise.

And I'm feigning for your touch,
we'll be each others crutch.
Just want to keep you in my clutch,
and I'm sorry if I'm a bit much.

But I don't want to wait,
I don't want to leave it up to fate.
Tell me, is there a way to perpetuate,
the love that we create?

~Long Distance Relationships

I don't like how we fight,
or how it can go on all night.
We supposed to shine bright,
instead we speak out of spite.

How are we going to grow,
when love we can't show?
Taking shots like three in a row,
when our pride we need to let go.

We should make each other smile,
instead of one of us feeling vile.
We say it's all worthwhile,
but differences we can't even reconcile.

We can't have a conversation,
without it spun into a confrontation.
We have good communication,
just poor interpretation.

Don't see the others perspective,
when clouded with our own objective.
Shouldn't be just corrective,
how about more protective?

We're at each other's throat,
are we even keeping Us afloat?
One's always the escape goat,
while the other seems to gloat.

Supposed to be them against us,
not hitting each other with the bus.
We can't help but fuss,
something's better left not discussed.

~Blind Love

Going into this New Years,
praying for less tears.
Leaving behind toxic peers,
real friends I'm taking volunteers.

Having this Ideation,
that to none I need an explanation.
Coming to the realization,
I control my reaction to every situation.

There is an endless range,
to make the needed change.
Love and Hate interchange,
to some its quite strange.

All smiles and no frown,
from now on I refuse to drown.
No more looking like a clown,
instead I'll put on the crown.

~ '2020'

I am blessed to say,
that I woke up today,
that I can feel the sun's ray,
and go outside and play.

Fortunate to be able to walk,
to converse and talk,
to relax and gawk,
and gaze at any flock.

Humbled to have the ability to eat,
to have socks to put on my feet,
to have multiple sources of heat,
a place to have a seat.

Grateful to have a place to rest,
being able to feel stress,
having ideas to manifest,
even just to look out to the west.

Lucky to have air to inhale,
To make mistakes and fail,
to have opportunity to prevail,
as well as not sitting in a cell.

~Gratitude

I smoke to keep on laughing,
making up for happiness I'm lacking.
Sometimes I just want to get a bae,
who loves to wake up and say,
That I'm a queen,
and a big part of their dream.
Someone who says to look in the mirror,
to open my eyes and see a little clearer.
Someone to take away the shame,
to calm the thoughts in my brain.
I admit I'm crazy,
But far from being lazy.
Can you relate,
To the words I articulate?
You will never understand,
Why the ground shakes where I stand.
Tired of all the smiles I must fake,
Can't stop knowing my minds at stake.
You aren't something I need,
feelings you gave me are replaced with weed.
So, I'll keep toking on this tree,
And focus on getting my degree.
As much as I want a bae,
To laugh and scream my name.
I can't because before we even start,
I can promise they'll break my heart.
I'll be left sitting all alone,
with no one to talk to on the phone.
I can fucking try,
but be left just wanting to die.
Instead I'll pick up these heavy books,
And when they walk by I won't even look.
Cause they just want relations,
instead I'll focus on my education.

~Priorities

I am reliable,
love undeniable.
Do you see the pain and glory,
that makes up my name and story?
I am charismatic,
when I speak you hear everything but static.
Do you feel the love I create,
can you handle its weight?
I am intelligent,
carry this heartbreak with elegance.
Do you taste the sugar in my words,
and understand the knowledge transferred?

~I am

Do you get joy,
from other's pain?
Is their heart a toy,
do you treat it as a game?
What's your intention,
is it filled with compassion?
Do you seek ascension,
or your own satisfaction?
Would you feel entitled,
To another's time?
Or is your pride too compiled,
To accept that as crime?

~Who are You?

For years,
I've been seeking freedom.
Pushing away my tears,
trying to build my kingdom.
Try to stay afloat,
looking for a place to call home.
My life I've rewrote,
but I don't want to roam.
I don't want to wander,
or be stuck in this place of in between.
To many hard decisions to ponder,
it's not as easy as it may seem.
Where do I even start,
trying to build my life?
Must protect my heart,
and stay away from strife.
See I know I have potential,
I could be someone great.
And of course, it's essential,
not to let another dictate.

~Where is Home?

Just know that me and you are not the same,
most of my demons I've overcame.
I don't live in shame,
I don't seek to place blame.

I strive for perfection,
and anything less is a defection.
Only time I turn to retrospection,
is when I'm off my path and need redirection.

People so quick to deceive,
if they even have a thought that you are naive.
And of course I know I shouldn't wear my heart on my sleeve,
because when times get hard everyone ready to leave.

See I'd rather pick myself up when I'm down,
and not depend on anyone to restraighten my crown.
I have to fix my own frown,
and keep my head up so I don't drown.

Constantly attempting to pray,
that I don't lead my priorities astray.
I put my aspirations on display,
and refuse any thought of dismay.

Most don't understand what I've had to undergo,
the expectations I've had to forgo.
The desires I've had to stow,
or why I can't let my pain show.

~Not the Same

She hears the whispers,
said behind her back.
All the snickers,
have turned her heart black.

People like to wonder,
why she's cold as ice.
She's been plundered,
of anything nice.

How does she walk,
with such grace?
How does she talk,
with a smile on her face?

She expects the tears,
to fall from her eyes.
She understands peers,
kiss her with lies.

So what keeps her,
from jumping you ask?
The pain she'll transfer,
to a drink in her flask.

Won't let them win,
she repeats everyday.
She lifts her chin,
and kneels to pray.

Her knees are weak,
And her hope's dying.
She's feeling bleak,
with her heart in hiding.

How does she arise,
when ready to collapse?
Pain will pressurize,
the desire to relapse.

A choice she'll make,
to decide her fate.
I hope for her sake,
She won't take the bait.

~What they did to her...

Do you treat the peasant,
the same as the king?
Do you do it in the present,
or only in the spring?

Do you open the door,
for the love of your life?
Do you feel it's a chore,
or does it turn into strife?

Do you house,
the people without a home?
Do you worry about your blouse,
or people without a comb?

Would you give,
the shoes off your feet?
Would you forgive,
the hardships of the street?

Would you smile,
to take someone's frown?
Would you reconcile,
or just put the other down?

Would you shoulder,
some of their pain?
Would you smolder,
or be more humane.

Would you lose,
so they can win?
Would you change views,
or feed the validation within?

~Underlying Intentions..

I see the pain,
hidden in your eyes.
I see the chain,
binding your cries.

Your smiles expose,
that you're hurt.
When I look to close,
your eyes avert.

You feel lonely,
even when not alone.
You're not the only,
just pick up the phone.

Cheering me up,
when you're the one down.
So I try to pick up,
that heartbreaking frown.

You've lost motivation,
to do everything.
But you have aspiration,
to be anything.

They did you wrong,
you say it's nothing new.
You're facade is strong,
but I see straight through.

Know from the start,
they'll disconcert.
You possess a heart,
that's bound to be hurt.

~I see you

She hugged her knees,
throat sore from her pleas.

God wasn't her savior,
from their vile behavior.

Now she can't sleep,
only just weep.

Scrubbing in the shower,
wishing away their power.

She wants to scream,
wake up from this dream.

She wants to escape,
from remembering the rape.

But there is no where,
no where without despair.

She can't think straight,
heart's burdened with hate.

To sleep take a few pills,
the darkness wills.

She had her sleep,
but sadly it was to deep.

Now people mourn her soul,
but wasn't this their goal?

What is love,
That's the question?
Is it a white dove,
or an obsession?

Neither of those,
it is a drug,
It's the aroma of a rose,
or coffee in a mug.

Love is having patience,
and understanding sacrifice.
Being gracious,
knowing what will suffice.

It's blindly jumping,
and falling hard.
It's being trusting,
putting down your guard.

Addicting more than less,
the withdraws exhausting.
It's overwhelming distress,
but can't help falling.

~THE DRUG

Can't contain the thoughts in my head,
the demons keep saying I would be better off dead.
Self hate is exactly what I'm trying to shed,
but I can barely drag myself out of bed.

And when I get in the shower I can't help but question if anyone will care,
because if they do why aren't they aware?
That its a constant struggle to keep my hips bare,
when really all I wanna do is cut and tear.

I'm attempting to fight,
to stay positive and keep my eyes on the light.
I used to be so bright,
but I guess somewhere I lost sight.

Terrified I'll end up in the grave,
because to my demons I'm their slave.
And to be honest the blade is what I crave,
but I won't lose this war and cave.

Scared of my emotions,
so I push them away and keep going through the motions.
But in my head there are to many commotions,
so many conflicting notions.

I would love to say I'm happy being me,
but it would be a lie to say I'm at that degree.
How do I set myself free,
where do I look for the key?

Keep wishing away this sense of demise,
but it can't hear me over my cries.
Behind my smile the pain underlies,
but one day my happiness is sure to monopolize.

But until then I'll try and prevail,
words of empowerment I'll make sure to inhale.
The demons I'll ship off in the mail,
and I know it's vital that I don't fail.

~Taunting

Happiness is a goal,
we strive to achieve.
It isn't something that can be stole,
that's just what we perceive.

It can't be controlled,
by an outside force.
It can't be sold,
that's out of its natural course.

We have the power,
to create happiness.
Even in the shower,
when your heart is full of sadness.

Take a step back,
put down the mask.
Put it with the stack,
of non-doable tasks.

Pick up the smile,
shake off the frown.
Get off the tile,
go out into town.

Sometimes there wont be a person,
cheering from the stands.
Don't let anyone worsen,
your emotions are in your hands.

~You're in control

You should know,
some things about me.
I love so hard it shows,
to the point its clear to see.

I will hold you down,
if you treat me like a queen.
I'll put on my crown,
and make you my king.

I need your attention,
for you to put up the same endeavor.
And it's worth a mention,
that to play me isn't clever.

I might need your validation,
that i'm really what you crave.
Show me appreciation,
and that you can behave.

I can be a bit much,
but i'll put you above.
I'll be that crutch,
and give you my love.

But if you try to hurt me,
you'll feel it ten times worse.
Play me and you'll see,
you'll wanna hit reverse.

~Know Me First

I'm tired of just trying to survive,
where is my will to live?
Why do I wanna die,
happiness is for what I strive.

I'm tired of begging myself not to give in,
to the darkness in my head.
How do I get back to who I used to have been,
instead of wanting to be dead?

The demons in my head are screaming,
telling me to hate my entire entity. They're feigning,
tearing apart my self love unrelentlessly.

I'm just trying to stay alive,
even when I wanna drown myself in a lake.
How do I survive,
when my smiles are almost always fake?

~Only Surviving

I know you feel like i'ma hurt you,
that you can't trust me.
But I promise that isn't true,
i'm tryna do everything for you to see.

Let me just paint you this illustration,
no matter what i'ma treat you as my king.
It shouldn't even be up for interpretation,
of course one day I hope for a ring.

I want to show you a different world,
of trust, love and loyalty.
I'm letting my guards be unfurled,
so I can show you another way without cruelty.

Because I'll do anything to see you smile,
just to see you happy and at ease.
I'll walk that extra mile,
because you're the person I want to please.

I know you think ima cheat,
but that's not the case.
What I'm saying is concrete,
you aren't someone I could replace.

I promise it's not even a temptation,
being with you is like living in the sky.
What we have can be a beautiful creation,
all I'm asking is for you to try.

We have that potential,
to prevail.
We aren't too differential,
there is always room to excel.

Just bare with me,
don't give up on us.
Because one day you'll see,
we're worth all the fuss.

~Worth It

You know I'm in pain,
trying to keep my head up and stay sane.
But of course my composure I'll maintain.
I'll submit and let you reign.

Just understand,
that I am not a person you can command.
There is only so much I can withstand,
you don't have to reprimand.

What happen to putting on my crown,
how did that turn to putting my down?
Crazy thing is that I don't want you to frown,
I do my best to make sure that you don't drown.

I try and take off the pressure,
even made sure I wasn't the stressor.
However I know I wasn't the aggressor,
and tried to show you the mind is a depressor.

I put up the endeavor,
our relationship I didn't want to sever.
I've wanted to keep you safe since forever,
but you won't control me whatsoever.

So I have to draw a line,
and hope one day the stars will realign.
Because without you I'm not fine,
but I have to make sure my mind doesn't decline.

Its natural for me to provide,
to just hush and put my own emotions aside.
I always put away my pride,
and when things got bad I was the one who complied.

To put on a smile became an obligation,
I painted the picture and showed you the illustration.
I laid out the interpretation,
but it wasn't enough and now we need separation.

-Had to let go

I'm on the brink,
of going insane.
Should I go see a shrink,
to take away the pain?

I need to foment,
a plan of change.
Pure intent ,
priorities I've had to rearrange.

I'm seeking joy,
in a world full of hate.
Thoughts aren't a toy,
they have the power to create.

-Losing It

Its like I'm losing you,
what the fuck am I supposed to do?
How do I cope,
it came time to say nope.

I can't keep letting you do this,
but you the one person I'll always miss.
But how many times have you cried,
how many times have I been by your side?

Don't forget I saved your life,
I noticed when you picked up a knife.
I held you down,
especially when I thought you would drown.

-I was always there

You wasted my time,
and broke my heart.
I'll be fine,
But i should've known from the start.
It was to good to be true,
no surprise we didn't last.
Your love you withdrew,
and became a nigga from my past.
How could you say,
you wouldn't give up on us?
I couldn't ask you to stay,
there was nothing left to discuss.
I guess i'm to much,
for you to handle.
You were supposed to be my crutch,
Instead for your failure i'll light a
candle.
You made me fall for you,
and give you my heart.
Why did you pursue,
when you knew from the start?
Why did you captivate,
my everyday thought?
Was it just to anticipate,
my level of distraught?
Why would you speak,
the most common lie?
It has me weak,
to intense to exemplify.
If this is how it feels to be loved,
it's not something i need.
But yes I had a crave of,
Us to succeed.

Instead I lay here,
missing our potential.
You played off my biggest fear,
were we to differential?
And I miss the knowing,
of you loving me.
But if you couldn't see us growing,
then we weren't meant to be.
To many times you uttered,
that you didn't wanna see me shed a
tear.
And my heart kinda stuttered,
When I understood you weren't sincere.
Did you ever care?
because I thought you were the best.
But I should've been aware,
that you are just like the rest.
You just wanted to play,
how long have you been lying?
But I wont portray,
how much i've been crying.
I hope you find your happiness,
even if it's not with me.
And for the moment i'll feel the
sadness,
but i'll always be strong like a tree.
I'll pray for you to prevail,
to grow and change.
Just know with me you failed,
and with your self you should be
ashamed.

~You lost 'The One'

See I wanna comfort your soul,
when the depression takes a toll.

I want you to be able to say,
that I was the one who would always stay.

I want to turn all of your fantasies,
into the realest realities.

You deserve that crown,
and not to be let down.

~The best

I love the way,
you lie.
How you say,
you can't see me cry.

So will you turn,
away from me?
Watching as I burn,
looking with envy.

Will you wipe,
away my tears?
I'm not your type,
on of my biggest fears.

~Burn

Got on my knees to pray,
begging God for a better day.
He didn't have anything to say,
left me feeling full of dismay.

Happiness I'm trying to expand,
but from that place I've been banned.
Only so much I can withstand,
pressure I know firsthand.

I don't wanna just survive,
rather learn to be alive.
Excellence is for what I strive,
happiness I need to revive.

~Discouraged

She seeks to disappear,
to leave behind her fear.
The damage to severe,
to ever persevere.

That's what she believes,
what she perceives.
The pain she relieves,
seep from under her sleeves.

Look away in shame,
curling inside her own frame.
Playing as if her life's a game,
looking at all she's overcame.

But is it enough,
is her life too rough?
Tired of acting tough,
and caring about stuff.

~The Aftermath

The weight of her absence,
or the toxic in her presence?

The miss of her touch,
or being her crutch?

yearning for a mother's love
or her wearing you like a glove.

~What's Worse?

Monsters live in my head,
not just under the bed.
The words they've said,
are full of dread.

They laugh at my pain,
keeping hope is a strain.
Having free reign,
insecurities their domain.

~2 p.m. Realizations

Be the demonstration,
that gives motivation.
Show a presentation,
that promotes innovation.

~Starts w/ You

About Poet

I'm everything but nothing.
I'm whole but empty.
I'm surrounded but alone.
I'm strong but weak.
I'm just me.

Contact:
bjas.internaldemons@aol.com
Also, I'd love if you would leave me a review.
breathe & exist

Made in the USA
Monee, IL
25 March 2020